frame>by>frame
italian

frame>by>frame
italian
a visual step-by-step cookbook

LOVE
FOOD™

First published in 2010
LOVE FOOD is an imprint of Parragon Books Ltd

Parragon
Queen Street House
4 Queen Street
Bath BA1 1HE, UK

ISBN: 978-1-4075-9093-6

Printed in China

Designed by Talking Design
Photography by Mike Cooper
Food styling by Lincoln Jefferson
New recipes by Christine France
Introduction by Linda Doeser

Notes for the Reader
This book uses imperial, metric, and US cup measurements. Follow the same units of measurement throughout; do not mix imperial and metric. All spoon measurements are level: teaspoons are assumed to be 5 ml, and tablespoons are assumed to be 15 ml. Unless otherwise stated, milk is assumed to be whole, eggs and individual vegetables are medium, and pepper is freshly ground black pepper.

The times given are an approximate guide only. Preparation times differ according to the techniques used by different people and the cooking times may also vary from those given. Optional ingredients, variations, or serving suggestions have not been included in the calculations.

Recipes using raw or very lightly cooked eggs should be avoided by infants, the elderly, pregnant women, convalescents, and anyone with a chronic illness. Pregnant and breast-feeding women are advised to avoid eating peanuts and peanut products. People with nut allergies should be aware that some of the prepared ingredients used in the recipes in this book may contain nuts. Always check the packaging before use.

contents

introduction

This magnificent cookbook with its wealth of beautiful and immensely useful photographs will prove to be an invaluable and delightful addition to any cook's bookshelf. The recipes are clear, easy to follow, superbly illustrated, delicious, and truly authentic, so whatever your level of expertise in the kitchen you are virtually guaranteed success every time.

Every recipe starts with a photograph of all the ingredients but this is more than just a pretty picture or—even less helpful—a montage that is not to scale so that an olive appears to be the same size as a lemon. Instead, it serves as a handy way of checking that you have everything ready before you start cooking. Just comparing the picture with the ingredients arranged on your own counter or kitchen table will ensure that you haven't left anything out and when it's time to add the parsley, for example, you have already chopped it as specified in the ingredients list. If you're uncertain about how thinly to slice tomatoes or how finely to dice eggplants, a glance at the photograph will provide an instant answer.

Each short and straightforward step of the method is clearly explained without any jargon or difficult technical terms. Once again, what you see in the photograph is what you should expect to see in front of you. Not only is this reassuring for the novice cook, but those with more experience will also find it a helpful reminder of the little touches that can easily be overlooked. Each recipe ends with a mouthwatering photograph of the finished dish, complete with any serving suggestions.

Why you need this book

Italian food is among the tastiest in the world and the Mediterranean diet is one of the healthiest. It is a varied cuisine that is popular with children and adults alike, making it the ideal choice for easy family meals. Its keynote is simplicity, but every dish is prepared with loving care to bring out the full flavor of each thoughtfully chosen ingredient.

In this book there are 60 fuss-free recipes that will enable you to re-create the authentic taste of Italy. You can simply pick and choose individual dishes for a quick and easy midweek supper or you can serve a formal Italian meal for a special occasion. This would start with soup or an antipasto (appetizer), followed by a first course of, say, pasta or risotto, then a second course of meat, poultry, or fish, and finish triumphantly with a fabulous sweet treat, such as a melt-in-the-mouth pastry or refreshing ice cream.

>1 >2 >3

>1 >2 >3

>4 >5 >6

top tips for success

> Simple dishes with relatively few ingredients require the freshest and best-quality produce. Ideally, buy vegetables and fruit in season.

> It is usually worth buying Italian brands of canned goods, rice, and pasta, because these will have been tried and tested in kitchens throughout Italy. Italian type 00 pasta flour is best for making pasta dough, but you can substitute it with all-purpose flour, if necessary.

> Always use olive oil, preferably an Italian one. The best-quality and most expensive is extra virgin, which is produced from the first cold pressing. Use this for salad dressings. Virgin oil is from the second pressing and is perfect for cooking. Oil simply labeled "pure" comes from the third or fourth pressing, will have been refined, and may have been treated with heat. The flavor is disappointing and it is best avoided.

> Always buy Parmesan cheese in a block and grate it freshly as required. Wrapped in wax paper, it keeps well in the refrigerator. Parmesan sold already grated is expensive and quickly loses its flavor.

> While dried pasta will keep more or less indefinitely, keep an eye on the expiration date of other pantry ingredients, such as flour, polenta, and nuts. Yeast loses its ability to ferment quite quickly, so if you're planning to make pizza, check the package. Spices also quickly lose their pungency, so buy them in small quantities and store in a cool, dark place.

> To cook perfect pasta, you will need 16 cups water and 3 tablespoons salt for every 10½ oz–1 lb/300–450 g dried or fresh pasta. The salt is essential to prevent the pasta from sticking; however very little, if any, salt is absorbed by the pasta. Bring the salted water to a boil in a large saucepan. You do not need to add any oil. Add the pasta, stir, and bring the water back to a boil before you start timing. Do not reduce the heat to low; the water must boil, not simmer. Cook unfilled dried pasta for 8–12 minutes and unfilled fresh pasta for 2–3 minutes. Cook filled dried pasta for 15–20 minutes and filled fresh pasta for 8–10 minutes. Drain the pasta in a colander or remove strands with a pasta fork or scoop. Pasta is best left damp rather than drained thoroughly. To test whether pasta is ready, break off a small piece with a fork and bite it between your front teeth. It should be "al dente," that is tender but still firm to the bite. It is advisable to start testing before you think the pasta will be ready.

> Polenta—the Italian version of grits—is made with a coarse, yellow cornmeal. Bring 5 cups salted water to a boil in a large saucepan. Gently sprinkle 1¼ cups yellow cornmeal into the pan with one hand while stirring vigorously with a wooden spoon with the other until all the cornmeal has been thoroughly incorporated. Italians cook traditional polenta over very low heat, stirring constantly, for 40–45 minutes, until the mixture comes away from the side of the pan. A quicker alternative is to use instant cornmeal, again stirring constantly, and cook for 10–15 minutes.

time-saving shortcuts

> Allow plenty of time for cooking and never try to rush things. Italians enjoy preparing food almost as much as they enjoy eating it and some dishes, notably risotto, require almost constant attention.

> To peel garlic, lightly crush a clove with the flat blade of a cook's knife. This makes the skin easy to remove.

> Use kitchen scissors to snip sun-dried tomatoes, prosciutto, pancetta, anchovy fillets, pitted olives, and fresh herbs rather than chopping with a knife.

> Tear salad greens and delicate herbs, such as basil, with your fingers rather than chopping them. It's quicker and prevents bruising.

> To peel tomatoes, peaches, and nectarines, slit the skins, put them into a heatproof bowl, and pour in boiling water to cover. Let stand for 30–60 seconds, then drain and peel. This also makes shallots easier to peel, but don't slit the skins first.

> To peel bell peppers, put them on a baking sheet and place under a preheated broiler for 10–15 minutes, turning occasionally. When they are blistered and charred, remove with tongs and transfer to a plastic bag. Tie the top and let stand until cool enough to handle, then untie the bag and peel off the skins.

> Put the ingredients for a salad dressing, such as a vinaigrette, into a screw-top jar, secure the lid, and shake vigorously.

> To make breadcrumbs, cut off the crusts and tear the bread into pieces, then add them to a food processor or blender through the feeder tube while the motor is running.

> If you will be using the oven or broiler, switch it on when you first go into the kitchen and before you start preparing the food. Ovens can take as long as 15 minutes to reach the required temperature.

>1 >2 >3

useful equipment

> **Saucepans:** A good set of heavy-bottom pans with tight-fitting lids is a worthwhile investment because they will last a lifetime if properly cared for. A range of sizes from small to large will ensure that you have the appropriate pan for the quantity of food you are cooking. Pasta, for example, requires a lot of water and a large pan to prevent it from sticking or boiling over. Similarly, you will need plenty of room to stir risotto because otherwise it is likely to spill all over the oven. Medium and small pans are ideal for vegetables and sauces. Using too large a pan may cause scorching and too small a pan will result in uneven cooking. Nonstick linings are a matter of personal choice.

> **Pasta pan:** This is a tall pan with an inner perforated container that lets you drain the pasta easily when cooked. It is not essential and may take up valuable storage space in the kitchen.

> **Colander:** Use a colander for draining pasta and salting vegetables, such as eggplants. Buy one that is at least 11 inches/28 cm in diameter and that has a sturdy base or legs so that it stands securely. Two handles make a large colander easier to lift. Colanders may be stainless steel, enameled, or plastic.

> **Skillet:** If you are buying only one, choose a large, heavy-bottom skillet. However, a medium-size skillet is a useful addition for cooking croûtons, omelets, or fish steaks.

> **Knives:** Good-quality, heavy, and well-balanced knives are essential in any kitchen. The minimum requirement is a paring, vegetable, utility, and cook's knife. Keep them sharpened using a V-sharpener, carborundum stone, or steel, and store them in a knife block. Sharp knives are not only easier to use, but are also safer because they are less liable to slip.

> **Mixing bowls:** A range of bowls is useful for arranging ingredients before you start cooking (small), beating eggs (medium), and making dough (large). Make sure that some are heatproof for melting chocolate and whisking egg custards over simmering water.

> **Pasta machine:** If you plan to make a lot of pasta dough yourself, this gadget makes easy work of the task of rolling it. Hand-cranked and electric machines are available and work on the same principle. Cut the dough into about 6 pieces. Wrap the pieces that you are not using immediately in plastic wrap to prevent them from drying out. Flatten one piece, fold it into 3, and pass it lengthwise through the rollers on the widest setting. Repeat the folding and rolling 3–4 times, then put the strip on a dish towel. Fold and roll the remaining pieces of dough in the same way, then close the rollers by one notch. Pass all the strips of dough through the machine again without folding. Continue rolling all the strips of dough, closing the rollers by one notch each time until you have used the narrowest setting. Do not be tempted to skip a notch. Attachments for cutting ribbons of different widths are available and other shapes may be cut by hand.

> **Rolling pin and pastry board:** You don't have to use a pasta machine to roll out the dough. It can be done with a rolling pin in much the same way as pastry dough. However, unlike pastry, pasta dough does not respond well to cold surfaces, so use a wooden board and rolling pin. You can just dust the surface with flour to prevent sticking, but using semolina results in a better, less floury flavor. Fold and roll pieces of dough, as for the pasta machine, to begin with and then roll out thinly and evenly. Wooden pasta rollers with variously sized cutting edges for hand-cutting pasta dough are available. Handle and store them carefully because they are fragile.

> **Ravioli mold:** This metal tray is divided into shallow squares with wide, flat edges between the indentations. It helps make ravioli all the same size and ensures that the edges are well sealed.

> **Ravioli cutter:** Like a cookie cutter with a handle, this makes stamping out dough for large ravioli easy.

> **Pasta wheel:** You can successfully use an ordinary pastry wheel for cutting pasta dough, but a wheel designed for pasta is usually heavier, ensuring a clean cut, and may have detachable wheels for plain and zigzag edges.

> **Mortar and pestle:** This tool is used to crush, grind, and mix ingredients, such as nuts. It is traditionally used to make pesto. The stick is called the pestle and the bowl is the mortar.

> **Strainers:** Fine-mesh, stainless steel strainers are invaluable for sifting flour, draining vegetables, straining sauces, and sprinkling unsweetened cocoa or confectioners' sugar over desserts. It is worth buying a nylon strainer for acidic mixtures, such as pureed fruit, which might be tainted by a metal strainer.

> **Graters:** A box grater is versatile with a choice of cutting surfaces that range from fine to coarse. It's sturdy and easy to use but takes up drawer space and it is sometimes tricky to remove all the raspings from inside. (Use a pastry brush.) A rotary grater is very safe and usually comes with several different cylinders for fine and coarse grating. It is the best choice for grating chocolate. Flat graters may have fine, medium, or coarse surfaces and it is best to buy them individually.

>1

>2

>3

antipasti

>4

>5

>6

ham & salami salad
with figs

serves 6

ingredients

6 ripe figs
6 thin slices prosciutto
12 thin slices salami

1 small bunch of fresh basil,
  separated into small sprigs
a few fresh mint sprigs
handful of arugula leaves

2 tbsp lemon juice
4 tbsp extra virgin olive oil
salt and pepper

> **1** Trim the stems of the figs to leave just a short length, then cut the figs into quarters.

> **2** Arrange the ham and salami on a large serving platter.

> **3** Wash and dry the herbs and arugula and put in a bowl with the prepared figs.

> **4** Whisk the lemon juice and oil together in a small bowl and season well with salt and pepper.

>5 Pour the lemon juice and oil mixture into the bowl with the herbs, arugula, and figs. Toss carefully until all the ingredients are well coated in the dressing.

>6 Spoon the figs and salad on top of the meat on the serving platter.

Serve immediately.

wild mushroom bruschetta

serves 4

ingredients

4 slices sourdough bread,
  such as Pugliese
3 garlic cloves, 1 halved
  and 2 finely chopped

3 tbsp extra virgin olive oil
8 oz/225 g mixed wild
  mushrooms, such as porcini,
  chanterelles, and portobello
  mushrooms

2 tbsp butter
1 small onion, finely chopped
4 tbsp white wine
salt and pepper

2 tbsp coarsely chopped fresh
  flat-leaf parsley, to garnish

>1 Preheat the broiler to medium. Toast the bread slices under the preheated broiler on both sides.

>2 Rub the bread with the garlic halves and drizzle with 2 tablespoons of the oil. Keep warm.

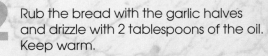

>3 Wipe the mushrooms thoroughly to remove any trace of soil and slice any large ones.

>4 Heat the remaining oil with half the butter in a skillet, add the mushrooms, and cook over medium heat, stirring, for 3–4 minutes, until soft. Remove with a slotted spoon and keep warm.

>5 Heat the remaining butter in the skillet.
Add the onion and chopped garlic and
cook, stirring, for 3–4 minutes, until soft.
Add the wine, stir, and let bubble
for 2–3 minutes, until reduced.

>6 Return the mushrooms
to the skillet and heat
through. The sauce should
be thick enough to glaze the
mushrooms. Season with salt
and pepper to taste.

Pile the mushrooms on top of the toasted bread, scatter over the parsley, and serve immediately.

fresh tomato soup with pasta

serves 4

ingredients

1 tbsp olive oil
4 large plum tomatoes
1 onion, cut into quarters
1 garlic clove, thinly sliced
1 celery stalk, coarsely
  chopped
generous 2 cups chicken stock
2 oz/55 g dried soup pasta
salt and pepper
chopped fresh flat-leaf parsley,
  to garnish

>1 Pour the oil into a large heavy-bottom saucepan and add the tomatoes, onion, garlic, and celery. Cover and cook over low heat, occasionally shaking gently, for 45 minutes, until pulpy.

>2 Transfer the mixture to a food processor or blender and process to a smooth puree.

Ladle into warmed bowls, sprinkle with parsley, and serve immediately.

>3 Push the puree through a strainer into a clean saucepan.

>4 Add the stock and bring to a boil. Add the pasta, bring back to a boil, and cook for 8–10 minutes, until the pasta is tender but still firm to the bite. Season with salt and pepper to taste.

green & white bean salad

serves 4

ingredients
½ cup cannellini beans,
  soaked overnight and
  drained

8 oz/225 g fine green beans,
  trimmed
¼ red onion, thinly sliced
12 pitted black olives
1 tbsp snipped fresh chives

dressing
½ tbsp lemon juice
½ tsp Dijon mustard
6 tbsp extra virgin olive oil
salt and pepper

1 Place the cannellini beans in a large saucepan. Cover with cold water and bring to a boil. Boil rapidly for 15 minutes, then reduce the heat and simmer for an additional 30 minutes, or until tender. Drain and set aside.

> **2** Meanwhile, plunge the green beans into a large pan of boiling water. Bring back to a boil and cook for 4 minutes, until just tender but still brightly colored. Drain and set aside.

> **3** Whisk together the dressing ingredients, seasoning with salt and pepper to taste, then let stand.

> **4** While both types of bean are still slightly warm, turn them into a shallow serving dish.

Scatter over the onion, olives, and chives.

>6 Whisk the dressing again and spoon
over the salad.

Serve at room temperature.

broiled mussels with parmesan, parsley & breadcrumbs

serves 4

ingredients

2 lb 4 oz/1 kg mussels
2 tbsp olive oil
2 shallots, finely chopped
1 garlic clove, crushed
4 tbsp dry white wine

¾ cup fresh white
  breadcrumbs
finely grated rind of 1 lemon
3 tbsp chopped fresh flat-leaf
  parsley

¼ cup finely grated Parmesan
  cheese
salt and pepper

>1 Preheat the broiler to high. Clean the mussels by scrubbing or scraping the shells and pull off any beards. Discard any with broken shells and any that refuse to close when tapped.

>2 Heat half the oil in a large pan and fry the shallots and garlic for 2–3 minutes, until softened. Add the mussels and wine, cover, and cook over high heat, shaking the pan, for 2–3 minutes, until the mussels have opened.

>3 Discard any mussels that remain closed. Drain the remaining mussels, reserving the cooking juices, and discard the top (empty) shells. If necessary, boil the juices to reduce to 3 tablespoons.

>4 Mix together the breadcrumbs, lemon rind, parsley, Parmesan, and the reserved cooking juices with salt and pepper to taste.

>5 Spoon a little of the breadcrumb mixture into each mussel half shell.

>6 Sprinkle the remaining oil over the mussels and cook under the preheated broiler for 2–3 minutes, until bubbling.

Transfer to a serving plate and serve immediately.

three-color salad

serves 4

ingredients
10 oz/280 g mozzarella cheese,
  drained
8 plum tomatoes
20 fresh basil leaves
½ cup extra virgin olive oil
salt and pepper

>1 Cut the mozzarella into thin slices.

>2 Cut the tomatoes into thin slices.

Serve immediately.

> **3** Arrange the cheese and tomato slices on 4 individual serving plates and season to taste with salt. Set aside in a cool place for 30 minutes.

> **4** Sprinkle the basil leaves over the salad, then drizzle with the oil and season with pepper to taste.

roasted bell peppers & tomatoes

serves 4

ingredients

2 red bell peppers
2 yellow bell peppers
2 orange bell peppers

4 tomatoes, halved
1 tbsp olive oil
3 garlic cloves, chopped
1 onion, sliced into rings

2 tbsp chopped fresh thyme
salt and pepper

>1 Preheat the broiler to medium. Halve and seed the bell peppers.

>2 Divide the bell peppers, cut-side down, between 2 baking sheets and cook under the preheated broiler for 10 minutes.

>3 Add the tomatoes to the baking sheets and broil for 5 minutes, until the skins of the bell peppers and tomatoes are charred.

>4 Put the bell peppers into a plastic bag for 10 minutes to sweat, which will make the skins easier to peel.

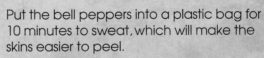

>**7** Heat the oil in a large skillet and fry the garlic and onion, stirring occasionally, for 3–4 minutes, or until softened.

>**8** Add the bell peppers and tomatoes to the skillet and cook for 5 minutes. Stir in the thyme and season with salt and pepper to taste.

Transfer to serving bowls and serve warm
or chilled.

traditional bean & cabbage soup

serves 6

ingredients

generous 1 cup dried
  cannellini beans, soaked
  overnight and drained
3 tbsp olive oil
2 red onions, coarsely chopped

4 carrots, sliced
4 celery stalks,
  coarsely chopped
4 garlic cloves,
  coarsely chopped
2½ cups vegetable stock

14 oz/400 g canned chopped
  tomatoes
2 tbsp chopped fresh
  flat-leaf parsley
1 lb 2 oz/500 g cavalo nero
  (black cabbage), thinly sliced

1 small 2-day-old ciabatta loaf,
  torn into small pieces
salt and pepper
extra virgin olive oil, to serve

>1 Place the beans in a large saucepan. Cover with cold water and bring to a boil, skimming off any foam. Reduce the heat and simmer, uncovered, for 1–1½ hours, until tender.

>2 Meanwhile, heat the olive oil in a large saucepan, add the onions, carrots, and celery, and cook over medium heat for 10–15 minutes, until softened. Add the garlic and cook for 1–2 minutes.

>3 Drain the beans, reserving the cooking water, and add half the beans to the pan. Add the stock, tomatoes, and parsley. Season well with salt and pepper.

>4 Bring to a simmer and cook, uncovered and stirring occasionally, for 30 minutes. Add the cabbage and cook, stirring occasionally, for an additional 15 minutes.

>5 Put the remaining beans in a food processor or blender with a little of the reserved cooking water and process to a smooth paste. Add to the soup.

 >6 Stir in the bread. The soup should be fairly thick; add more of the reserved cooking water to thin if necessary.

Ladle into warmed bowls, drizzle over a little extra virgin olive oil, and serve immediately.

zucchini frittata

serves 4–6

ingredients
1 red onion
4 zucchini
3 tbsp olive oil
1 garlic clove, finely chopped
5 large eggs
4 tbsp chopped fresh
  flat-leaf parsley
salt and pepper

> **>1** Preheat the broiler to high. Thinly slice the onion and cut the zucchini into ½-inch/ 1-cm dice.

> **>2** Heat the oil in a skillet. Fry the onions, zucchini, and garlic gently, stirring occasionally, until softened.

Cut the frittata into wedges
and serve warm or cold.

>3 Beat the eggs with salt and pepper to
taste, then stir into the pan with the parsley.
Cook over low heat for about 10 minutes,
until almost set.

>4 Cook the frittata under the preheated broiler
until the top is set and bubbling.

florentine-style crostini

serves 6

ingredients

6 slices ciabatta bread
2 garlic cloves, 1 halved
   and 1 crushed
2 tbsp extra virgin olive oil
3 tbsp olive oil

1 onion, chopped
1 celery stalk, chopped
1 carrot, chopped
4½ oz/125 g chicken livers
4½ oz/125 g calf, lamb,
   or pig liver

⅔ cup red wine
1 tbsp tomato paste
2 tbsp chopped fresh flat-leaf
   parsley
3–4 canned anchovy fillets,
   drained and finely chopped

2 tbsp water
2–3 tbsp butter
1 tbsp capers
salt and pepper

>**1** Preheat the broiler to medium. Toast the bread slices under the preheated broiler on both sides.

>**2** Rub the bread with the garlic halves and drizzle with the extra virgin olive oil. Transfer to a baking sheet and keep warm.

>**3** Heat the olive oil in a pan, then add the onion, celery, carrot, and crushed garlic. Cook gently for 4–5 minutes, or until the onion is soft but not colored.

>**4** Meanwhile, rinse and dry the chicken livers. Rinse and dry the calf liver and slice into strips.

>5 Add the liver to the pan and fry gently for a few minutes, until well sealed on all sides. Add half of the wine and cook until it has mostly evaporated.

>6 Add the remaining wine, the tomato paste, half the parsley, the anchovies, water, a little salt, and plenty of pepper. Cover and simmer, stirring occasionally, for 15–20 minutes, until most of the liquid has been absorbed.

>7 Let cool slightly, then transfer to a food processor and process to a chunky puree.

>8 Return to the pan and add the butter, capers, and the remaining parsley. Heat gently until the butter melts. Adjust the seasoning, adding salt and pepper if needed.

Serve warm or cold spread on the toasted bread.

arugula & parmesan salad with pine nuts

serves 4

ingredients

2 handfuls of arugula leaves
1 small fennel bulb
5 tbsp olive oil

2 tbsp balsamic vinegar
3½ oz/100 g Parmesan cheese
⅓ cup pine nuts
salt and pepper

Wash the arugula, discarding any wilted leaves or coarse stems, and pat dry. Divide among 4 serving plates.

Halve the fennel bulb and slice it finely. Arrange the sliced fennel over the arugula.

Whisk together the oil and vinegar with salt and pepper to taste. Drizzle a little of the dressing over each serving.

Cut the Parmesan into thin shavings using a knife or vegetable peeler.

>5 Toast the pine nuts in a dry skillet until golden brown.

>6 Top the salad with the Parmesan shavings and toasted pine nuts.

Serve immediately.

marinated raw beef

serves 4

ingredients

7 oz/200 g beef tenderloin,
  in one piece
2 tbsp lemon juice
4 tbsp extra virgin olive oil
2 oz/55 g Parmesan cheese,
  cut into thin shavings
4 tbsp chopped fresh
  flat-leaf parsley
salt and pepper
lemon slices, to garnish
crusty bread, to serve

>1 Using a very sharp knife, cut the beef tenderloin into wafer-thin slices and arrange on 4 serving plates.

>2 Pour the lemon juice into a small bowl and whisk in the oil. Season with salt and pepper to taste.

Garnish with lemon slices and serve with bread.

>3 Pour the dressing over the beef. Cover the plates with plastic wrap and let marinate for 10–15 minutes.

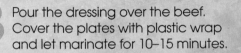

>4 Remove and discard the plastic wrap. Arrange the Parmesan shavings in the center of each serving and sprinkle with the parsley.

potato & pasta soup with pesto

serves 4

ingredients

1 lb/450 g floury potatoes
3 slices pancetta, chopped
2 tbsp olive oil
1 lb/450 g onions, finely
  chopped
2½ cups chicken stock
2½ cups milk

3½ oz/100 g dried conchigliette
⅔ cup heavy cream
2 tbsp chopped fresh flat-leaf
  parsley
salt and pepper
Parmesan cheese shavings,
  to serve

pesto

1 cup fresh flat-leaf parsley
  leaves
2 garlic cloves, chopped
generous ⅓ cup pine nuts
2 tbsp chopped fresh basil
  leaves

½ cup grated Parmesan
  cheese
⅔ cup olive oil

> 1 To make the pesto, put all of the ingredients in a food processor or blender and process for 2 minutes, or blend by hand using a mortar and pestle.

> 2 Peel the potatoes and finely chop.

> 3 Cook the pancetta in a large saucepan over medium heat for 4 minutes. Add the oil, potatoes, and onions and cook, stirring constantly, for 12 minutes.

> 4 Add the stock and milk to the pan, bring to a boil, and simmer for 10 minutes.

>5 Add the pasta and simmer for an additional 10–12 minutes, or according to the cooking time given in the package directions.

>6 Stir in the cream and simmer for 5 minutes. Add the chopped parsley and 2 tablespoons of the pesto. Season with salt and pepper to taste.

Ladle the soup into serving bowls and serve with Parmesan shavings.

sardines with pine nuts & raisins

serves 4

ingredients

1 small red onion, thinly sliced
1 tbsp olive oil
4 tbsp lemon juice
⅓ cup raisins

4 tbsp chopped fresh flat-leaf
 parsley, plus extra to garnish
generous ⅓ cup pine nuts,
 lightly toasted, plus extra
 to garnish

8–12 fresh sardines, cleaned
 and heads removed
salt and pepper

> **1** Preheat the oven to 400°F/200°C. Place the onion in a pan with the oil and 3 tablespoons of the lemon juice.

> **2** Cook gently, stirring, for 2–3 minutes, until the onion is softened. Remove from the heat and stir in the raisins.

> **3** Add the parsley and pine nuts to the onion mixture.

> **4** Place the sardines on a board, backbone uppermost, and press firmly along the backbone with your thumb. Turn over and remove the bones.

> **6** Arrange the sardines in a single layer in a shallow ovenproof dish, season with salt and pepper to taste, and sprinkle with the remaining lemon juice. Bake in the preheated oven for about 10 minutes.

Serve warm or cold, sprinkled with pine nuts
and parsley.

hot anchovy & garlic dip

serves 4

ingredients
3 tbsp unsalted butter
3 garlic cloves, crushed
6 salted anchovy fillets, rinsed
⅔ cup olive oil
raw vegetables, such as bell
  peppers, celery, fennel, and
  scallions, to serve

>1 Place the butter and garlic in a small heavy-bottom saucepan over low heat, stirring until the butter melts.

>2 Cook gently, stirring, for an additional 2 minutes, until the garlic is soft but not browned.

Serve the dip hot with the
vegetables on the side.

3 Add the anchovies and oil, then heat
gently, stirring, until the anchovies dissolve
into the oil and the sauce is creamy.

>4 Prepare the vegetables, cut into strips, and
arrange on a large platter.

>1

>2

>3

first course

>4

>5

>6

tagliatelle with a rich meat sauce

serves 4

ingredients

4 tbsp olive oil, plus extra
  for drizzling
3 oz/85 g pancetta or lean
  bacon, diced
1 onion, chopped

1 garlic clove, finely chopped
1 carrot, chopped
1 celery stalk, chopped
8 oz/225 g fresh ground beef
4 oz/115 g chicken livers,
  chopped

2 tbsp pureed canned
  tomatoes
½ cup dry white wine
1 cup beef stock
1 tbsp chopped fresh oregano
1 bay leaf

1 lb/450 g dried tagliatelle
salt and pepper
grated Parmesan cheese,
  to serve

>1 Heat the oil in a large heavy-bottom saucepan. Add the pancetta and cook over medium heat, stirring occasionally, for 3–5 minutes, until it is just turning brown.

>2 Add the onion, garlic, carrot, and celery and cook, stirring occasionally, for an additional 5 minutes.

>3 Add the beef and cook over high heat, breaking up the meat with a wooden spoon, for 5 minutes, until browned.

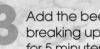

>4 Stir in the chicken livers and cook, stirring occasionally, for an additional 2–3 minutes.

>**5** Add the pureed tomatoes, wine, stock, oregano, and bay leaf and season with salt and pepper to taste. Bring to a boil, reduce the heat, cover, and simmer for 30–35 minutes.

>**6** Meanwhile, bring a large saucepan of lightly salted water to a boil. Add the pasta, bring back to a boil, and cook for 8–10 minutes, or according to the package directions, until tender but still firm to the bite.

>**7** Drain the pasta and transfer to a warmed serving dish. Drizzle with a little oil and toss well.

>**8** Remove and discard the bay leaf from the sauce, then pour the sauce over the pasta and toss again.

Serve immediately with grated
Parmesan.

chicken risotto with saffron

serves 4

ingredients

9 tbsp butter
2 lb/900 g skinless, boneless
  chicken breasts, thinly sliced
1 large onion, chopped

2½ cups risotto rice
⅔ cup white wine
1 tsp crumbled saffron
  threads
5¼ cups hot chicken stock

½ cup Parmesan cheese,
  grated
salt and pepper

> **1** Heat half of the butter in a deep saucepan. Add the chicken and onion and cook, stirring frequently, for 8 minutes, or until golden brown.

> **2** Add the rice and mix to coat in the butter. Cook, stirring constantly, for 2–3 minutes, or until the grains are translucent.

> **3** Add the wine and cook, stirring constantly, for 1 minute, until reduced.

> **4** Mix the saffron with 4 tablespoons of the hot stock. Add the liquid to the rice and cook, stirring constantly, until it is absorbed.

>5 Gradually add the remaining hot stock, a ladleful at a time. Add more liquid as the rice absorbs each addition. Cook, stirring, for 20 minutes, or until all the liquid is absorbed and the rice is creamy.

>6 Remove from the heat and add the remaining butter. Mix well, then stir in the Parmesan until it melts. Season with salt and pepper to taste.

Spoon the risotto into warmed serving dishes and serve immediately.

macaroni with chickpeas, herbs & garlic

serves 4

ingredients

12 oz/350 g dried short-cut
  macaroni
3 tbsp olive oil
1 onion, finely chopped
1 garlic clove, crushed
14 oz/400 g canned chickpeas,
  drained
4 tbsp pureed canned
  tomatoes
2 tbsp chopped fresh oregano
small handful of basil leaves,
  shredded, plus extra sprigs
  to garnish
salt and pepper

>**1** Bring a saucepan of lightly salted water to
a boil. Add the pasta, bring back to a boil,
and cook for 8–10 minutes, or according to
the package directions, until tender but still
firm to the bite. Drain well.

>**2** Meanwhile, heat the oil in a pan
and fry the onion and garlic, stirring
occasionally, for 4–5 minutes, until
golden.

Serve the pasta in wide dishes, garnished with basil sprigs.

>3 Add the chickpeas and pureed tomatoes to the pan and stir until heated through.

>4 Stir the pasta into the pan with the oregano and shredded basil. Season with salt and pepper to taste.

cannelloni with spinach & ricotta

serves 4

ingredients
melted butter, for greasing
12 dried cannelloni tubes, each
    about 3 inches/7.5 cm long
salt and pepper

filling
5 oz/140 g frozen spinach,
    thawed and drained
½ cup ricotta cheese
1 egg
3 tbsp grated pecorino cheese
pinch of freshly grated nutmeg

cheese sauce
2 tbsp butter
2 tbsp all-purpose flour
2½ cups hot milk
¾ cup grated Gruyère cheese

> **1** Preheat the oven to 350°F/180°C. Grease a rectangular ovenproof dish with the melted butter.

> **2** Bring a large saucepan of lightly salted water to a boil. Add the cannelloni tubes, bring back to a boil, and cook for 6–7 minutes, or according to the package directions, until nearly tender. Drain and rinse, then spread out on a clean dish towel.

> **3** For the filling, put the spinach and ricotta into a food processor and process briefly until combined. Add the egg and pecorino and process to a smooth paste. Transfer to a bowl, add the nutmeg, and season with salt and pepper to taste.

> **4** Spoon the filling into a piping bag fitted with a ½-inch/1-cm tip. Carefully open a cannelloni tube and pipe in a little of the filling. Place the filled tube in the prepared dish and repeat.

>5 For the cheese sauce, melt the butter in a saucepan. Add the flour to the butter and cook over low heat, stirring constantly, for 1 minute.

>6 Remove from the heat and gradually stir in the hot milk. Return to the heat and bring to a boil, stirring constantly. Simmer over low heat, stirring frequently, for 10 minutes, until thickened and smooth.

>7 Remove from the heat, stir in the Gruyère, and season with salt and pepper to taste.

>8 Spoon the cheese sauce over the filled cannelloni. Cover the dish with foil and bake in the preheated oven for 20–25 minutes.

Serve immediately.

broiled polenta with fennel seeds

serves 4

ingredients

4 cups water
1⅔ cups instant cornmeal
2 tbsp butter
1 tbsp fennel seeds

2 tbsp finely chopped
 fresh flat-leaf parsley
olive oil, for brushing
salt and pepper

>1 Place the water in a pan, add salt to taste, and bring to a boil. Sprinkle in the cornmeal, stirring.

>2 Stir over medium heat for 10–15 minutes, or according to the package directions, until the cornmeal thickens and comes away from the sides of the pan.

>3 Remove from the heat and stir in the butter, fennel seeds, and parsley. Season with pepper to taste.

>4 Brush a rectangular ovenproof dish with oil. Spoon the cornmeal mixture into the prepared dish, spread the surface level, and let set.

>5 Preheat the broiler to high. When set, turn out the polenta and cut into slices.

>6 Brush the polenta slices with oil and place under the preheated broiler until browned and crispy.

Serve immediately. This makes an excellent accompaniment to broiled Tuscan sausages or fish dishes.

risotto with peas & gorgonzola

serves 4

ingredients

2 tbsp olive oil
2 tbsp butter
1 onion, finely chopped
1 garlic clove, finely chopped
1¾ cups risotto rice
⅔ cup dry white wine
5¼ cups hot vegetable stock
2⅔ cups frozen peas
1 cup crumbled Gorgonzola
  cheese
2 tbsp chopped fresh mint
salt and pepper

>1 Heat the oil and butter in a deep saucepan. Add the onion and cook, stirring frequently, for 3–4 minutes, until softened.

>2 Add the garlic and rice and mix to coat in the butter and oil. Cook, stirring constantly, for 2–3 minutes, or until the grains are translucent. Add the wine and cook, stirring constantly, for 1 minute, until reduced.

Serve the risotto immediately.

>3 Gradually add the hot stock, a ladleful at a time. Cook, stirring, for 15 minutes, then stir in the peas and cook for an additional 5 minutes, until the liquid is absorbed and the rice is creamy.

>4 Remove from the heat. Stir in the Gorgonzola and mint, then season with salt and pepper to taste.

ravioli with crabmeat & ricotta

serves 4

ingredients
scant 2½ cups type 00 pasta
   flour or all-purpose flour
1 tsp salt
3 eggs, beaten
5 tbsp butter, melted

filling
6 oz/175 g white crabmeat
¾ cup ricotta cheese
finely grated rind of 1 lemon
pinch of dried chile flakes

2 tbsp chopped fresh flat-leaf
   parsley
salt and pepper

>1 Sift the flour and salt onto a board or work surface, make a well in the center, and add the eggs.

>2 Stir with a fork to gradually incorporate the flour into the liquid to form a dough.

>3 Knead for about 5 minutes, until the dough is smooth. Wrap in plastic wrap and let rest for 20 minutes.

>4 For the filling, stir together the crabmeat, ricotta, lemon rind, chile flakes, and parsley. Season with salt and pepper to taste.

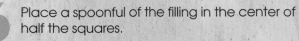

>**5** Roll the dough with a pasta machine or by hand to a thickness of about ⅛ inch/ 3 mm and cut into thirty-two 2½-inch/ 6-cm squares.

>**6** Place a spoonful of the filling in the center of half the squares.

>**7** Brush the edges with water and place the remaining squares on top, pressing to seal.

>**8** Bring a saucepan of lightly salted water to a boil. Add the ravioli, bring back to a boil, and cook for about 3 minutes, until tender but still firm to the bite. Drain well.

Drizzle the melted butter over the ravioli, sprinkle with pepper, and serve immediately.

cheese & tomato pizza

serves 2

ingredients
pizza dough
1¾ cups all-purpose flour, plus
   extra for dusting
1 tsp salt

1 tsp active dry yeast
1 tbsp olive oil, plus extra for
   oiling
6 tbsp lukewarm water

topping
6 tomatoes, thinly sliced
6 oz/175 g mozzarella cheese,
   drained and thinly sliced
2 tbsp shredded fresh basil

2 tbsp olive oil
salt and pepper

>1 To make the pizza dough, sift the flour and salt into a bowl and stir in the yeast. Make a well in the center and pour in the oil and water.

>2 Gradually incorporate the dry ingredients into the liquid, using floured hands. Turn out the dough onto a lightly floured surface and knead for 5 minutes, until smooth and elastic.

>3 Return the dough to a clean bowl, cover with lightly oiled plastic wrap, and let rise in a warm place for about 1 hour, or until doubled in size.

>4 Preheat the oven to 450°F/230°C. Lightly oil a baking sheet.

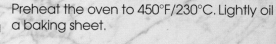

5 Turn out the dough onto a lightly floured surface and punch down. Knead briefly, then roll out into a round about ¼ inch/5 mm thick.

>6 Transfer to the prepared baking sheet and push up the edges with your fingers to form a small rim.

>7 For the topping, arrange the tomato and mozzarella slices over the pizza crust.

>8 Season with salt and pepper to taste, sprinkle with the basil, and drizzle with the oil. Bake in the preheated oven for 20–25 minutes, until golden brown.

Cut into slices and serve immediately.

pappardelle with cherry tomatoes, arugula & mozzarella

serves 4

ingredients
14 oz/400 g dried pappardelle
2 tbsp olive oil
1 garlic clove, chopped
12 oz/350 g cherry tomatoes,
  halved
3 oz/85 g arugula leaves
10½ oz/300 g mozzarella
  cheese, drained and cubed
salt and pepper
grated Parmesan cheese,
  to serve

>1 Bring a large saucepan of lightly salted water to a boil. Add the pasta, bring back to a boil, and cook for 8–10 minutes, or according to the package directions, until tender but still firm to the bite.

>2 Meanwhile, heat the oil in a skillet over medium heat and fry the garlic, stirring, for 1 minute, without browning.

Serve the pasta in wide dishes, sprinkled with Parmesan.

>3 Add the tomatoes, season well with salt and pepper, and cook gently for 2–3 minutes, until softened.

>4 Drain the pasta and stir into the skillet. Add the arugula leaves and mozzarella, then stir until the leaves wilt.

stuffed risotto balls

serves 3–4

ingredients

1 tbsp olive oil
3 tbsp butter
1 small onion, finely chopped
2¼ cups risotto rice

8 cups hot vegetable stock
½ cup grated Parmesan
  cheese
4 oz/115 g mozzarella cheese,
  drained and cubed
1 egg, beaten

2 cups fresh breadcrumbs
oil, for deep-frying
salt and pepper

>1 Heat the oil with 2 tablespoons of the butter in a deep saucepan. Add the onion and cook, stirring frequently, for 5 minutes, or until softened.

>2 Add the rice and mix to coat in oil and butter. Cook, stirring constantly, for 2–3 minutes, or until the grains are translucent.

>3 Gradually add the hot stock, a ladleful at a time. Add more liquid as the rice absorbs each addition. Cook, stirring, for 20 minutes, or until all the liquid is absorbed and the rice is creamy.

>4 Remove from the heat and add the remaining butter. Mix well, then stir in the Parmesan until it melts. Season with salt and pepper to taste. Let cool completely.

>5 Place 1 tablespoon of the risotto in the palm of your hand. Top with a cube of mozzarella, then place another tablespoon of risotto on top. Press together to form a ball, making sure that the filling is fully enclosed. Repeat until all the risotto and mozzarella have been used up.

>6 Chill the risotto balls for 10 minutes, then dip in the egg. Drain and coat in the breadcrumbs, shaking off any excess. Chill for 10 minutes.

>7 Heat enough oil for deep-frying in a large saucepan or deep-fat fryer to 350–375°F/180–190°C, or until a cube of bread browns in 30 seconds. Carefully drop in the risotto balls, in batches, and cook for 5 minutes, until golden brown.

>8 Remove the risotto balls from the oil with a slotted spoon, then drain on paper towels.

Let cool slightly before serving.

potato gnocchi with walnut pesto

serves 4

ingredients

1 lb/450 g floury potatoes
½ cup grated Parmesan
  cheese

1 egg, beaten
1⅔ cups all-purpose flour, plus
  extra for dusting
salt and pepper

walnut pesto

⅔ cup fresh flat-leaf parsley
2 tbsp capers, rinsed
2 garlic cloves, crushed

¾ cup extra virgin olive oil
½ cup chopped walnuts
⅓ cup grated pecorino or
  Parmesan cheese

> 1 Cook the potatoes in their skins in a large saucepan of boiling water for 30–35 minutes, until tender. Drain well and let cool slightly.

> 2 Meanwhile, put all of the pesto ingredients in a food processor or blender and process for 2 minutes, or blend by hand using a mortar and pestle.

> 3 When the potatoes are cool enough to handle, peel off their skins and pass the flesh through a strainer into a large bowl or press through a potato ricer.

> 4 Season well with salt and pepper and add the Parmesan. Beat in the egg and sift in the flour.

5 Lightly mix together, then turn out onto a lightly floured work surface. Knead lightly to form a smooth dough. If it is too sticky, add a little more flour.

>6 Roll out the dough into a long log. Cut into 1-inch/2.5-cm pieces and gently press with a fork to create the traditional ridged effect.

>7 Transfer to a floured baking sheet and cover with a clean dish towel until you are ready to cook.

>8 Bring a large saucepan of water to a boil, add the gnocchi, in batches, and cook for 1–2 minutes. Remove with a slotted spoon and transfer to a warmed serving dish.

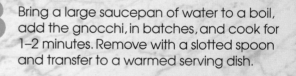

Serve immediately, topped with
the pesto.

linguine with anchovies, olives & capers

serves 4

ingredients
3 tbsp olive oil
2 garlic cloves, finely chopped
10 anchovy fillets, drained and
    chopped
¾ cup pitted and chopped
    black olives
1 tbsp capers, rinsed
1 lb/450 g plum tomatoes,
    peeled, seeded, and
    chopped
cayenne pepper, to taste
14 oz/400 g dried linguine
salt
2 tbsp chopped fresh flat-leaf
    parsley, to garnish

>1 Heat the oil in a heavy-bottom saucepan.
Add the garlic and cook over low heat,
stirring frequently, for 2 minutes. Add the
anchovies and mash them to a pulp
with a fork.

>2 Add the olives, capers, and tomatoes
and season with cayenne pepper
to taste. Cover and simmer for
25 minutes.

Garnish with the parsley and serve immediately.

>3 Meanwhile, bring a saucepan of lightly salted water to a boil. Add the pasta, bring back to a boil, and cook for 8–10 minutes, or according to the package directions, until tender but still firm to the bite.

>4 Drain the pasta and transfer to a warmed serving dish. Spoon the anchovy sauce into the dish and toss the pasta, using 2 large forks.

chicken & mushroom lasagna

serves 4–6

ingredients
2 tbsp olive oil

1 large onion, finely chopped

1 lb 2 oz/500 g fresh ground chicken or turkey

3½ oz/100 g smoked pancetta, chopped

3½ cups chopped cremini mushrooms

3½ oz/100 g dried porcini mushrooms, soaked

⅔ cup dry white wine

14 oz/400 g canned chopped tomatoes

3 tbsp chopped fresh basil leaves

9 sheets dried lasagna

3 tbsp finely grated Parmesan cheese

salt and pepper

white sauce
2½ cups milk

4 tbsp butter

scant ½ cup all-purpose flour

1 bay leaf

> **1** Preheat the oven to 375°F/190°C. For the white sauce, heat the milk, butter, flour, and bay leaf in a pan, whisking constantly, until smooth and thick. Season with salt and pepper to taste, cover, and let stand.

> **2** Heat the oil in a large saucepan and fry the onion, stirring, for 3–4 minutes.

> **3** Add the chicken and pancetta and cook for 6–8 minutes. Stir in both types of mushrooms and cook for an additional 2–3 minutes.

> **4** Add the wine and bring to a boil. Pour in the tomatoes, cover, and simmer for 20 minutes. Stir in the basil.

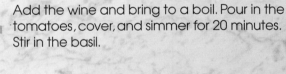

5 Meanwhile, bring a large saucepan of lightly salted water to a boil. Add the lasagna sheets, bring back to a boil, and cook according to the package directions. Drain well on a clean dish towel.

 **6** Arrange 3 of the lasagna sheets in a rectangular ovenproof dish, then spoon over a third of the meat sauce.

 7 Remove and discard the bay leaf from the white sauce. Spread a third of the sauce over the meat. Repeat the layers twice more, finishing with a layer of white sauce.

 8 Sprinkle with the Parmesan and bake in the preheated oven for 35–40 minutes, until the topping is golden brown and bubbling.

Serve immediately.

seafood risotto

serves 4

ingredients

⅔ cup dry white wine

4 baby squid, cleaned and sliced

9 oz/250 g shrimp, peeled and deveined

9 oz/250 g mussels, scrubbed and debearded

2 tbsp olive oil

4 tbsp butter

1 onion, finely chopped

2 garlic cloves, finely chopped

2 bay leaves

1¾ cups risotto rice

about 6 cups hot fish stock

salt and pepper

chopped fresh flat-leaf parsley, to garnish

>1 Heat the wine in a saucepan until boiling, add the squid and shrimp, cover, and cook for 2 minutes. Remove the squid and shrimp with a slotted spoon and set aside.

>2 Discard any mussels with broken shells and any that refuse to close when tapped. Add the mussels to the pan, cover, and cook for 2–3 minutes, until they have opened. Discard any that remain closed. Drain the mussels, reserving the juices, and remove the meat from the shells.

>3 Heat the oil and butter in a deep saucepan. Add the onion and cook, stirring frequently, for 3–4 minutes, until softened.

>4 Add the garlic, bay leaves, and rice, and mix to coat in the butter and oil. Cook, stirring constantly, for 2–3 minutes, until the grains are translucent.

>5 Stir in the cooking juices from the mussels, then gradually add the hot stock, a ladleful at a time. Cook, stirring, for 15 minutes, until the liquid is absorbed and the rice is creamy.

>6 Stir in the cooked seafood, cover, and cook for an additional 2 minutes to heat through. Season with salt and pepper to taste.

Serve the risotto immediately, sprinkled with parsley.

pizza turnovers

serves 4

ingredients
2 quantities pizza dough
  (see page 92)
all-purpose flour, for dusting

filling
2 tbsp olive oil, plus extra for
  oiling
1 red onion, thinly sliced
1 garlic clove, finely chopped
14 oz/400 g canned chopped
  tomatoes
⅓ cup pitted black olives
7 oz/200 g mozzarella cheese,
  drained and diced
1 tbsp chopped fresh oregano

1 Preheat the oven to 400°F/200°C. Lightly
oil 2 baking sheets. Heat the oil in a skillet.
Add the onion and garlic and cook for
5 minutes, until softened. Add the tomatoes
and cook for an additional 5 minutes. Stir
in the olives.

>2 Divide the dough into 4 pieces.
Roll out each piece on a lightly
floured surface to form an 8-inch/
20-cm round.

Let stand for 2 minutes
before serving.

> **>3** Divide the tomato mixture among the rounds, spreading it over half of each almost to the edge. Sprinkle over the mozzarella and oregano. Brush the edges of the rounds with a little water, then fold in half and press to seal.

> **>4** Transfer the turnovers to the prepared baking sheets and bake in the preheated oven for about 15 minutes, until golden and crispy.

>1

>2

>3

second course

>4   >5   >6

veal with prosciutto & sage

serves 4

ingredients

4 veal scallops
2 tbsp lemon juice
1 tbsp chopped fresh
  sage leaves

4 slices prosciutto
4 tbsp butter
3 tbsp dry white wine
salt and pepper

>1 Place the veal scallops between 2 sheets of plastic wrap and pound with a rolling pin until they are very thin.

>2 Transfer to a plate and sprinkle with the lemon juice. Set aside for 30 minutes, spooning the juice over them occasionally.

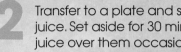

>3 Pat the scallops dry with paper towels, season well with salt and pepper, and rub with half the sage. Place a slice of prosciutto on each scallop and secure with a toothpick.

>4 Melt the butter in a large heavy-bottom skillet. Add the remaining sage and cook over low heat, stirring constantly, for 1 minute.

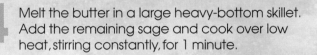

121

5

Add the scallops, in batches if necessary, and cook for 3–4 minutes on each side, until golden brown. Pour in the wine and cook for an additional 2 minutes.

>6 Transfer the scallops to warmed serving plates and pour the pan juices over them. Remove and discard the toothpicks.

Serve immediately.

monkfish skewers with basil mayonnaise

serves 2–4

ingredients

1 garlic clove, crushed
finely grated rind and juice
    of 1 lemon
2 tbsp olive oil

1 lb 2 oz/500 g monkfish fillet,
    cut into 1¼-inch/3-cm chunks
2 red onions, cut into thin
    wedges
salt and pepper

basil mayonnaise

2 egg yolks
1 tbsp lemon juice
1 tsp Dijon mustard
⅔ cup sunflower oil

⅔ cup extra virgin
    olive oil
1⅓ cups chopped fresh basil
    leaves

>1 Mix the garlic, lemon rind and juice, and olive oil with salt and pepper to taste. Stir in the fish, cover, and let marinate in the refrigerator for 30 minutes.

>2 If using wooden skewers, soak them in water for 30 minutes. For the basil mayonnaise, whisk together the egg yolks, lemon juice, and mustard until smooth.

>3 Very gradually whisk in the sunflower oil until the mixture thickens.

>4 Whisk in the extra virgin olive oil in a thin, steady stream to make a thick, creamy sauce. Stir in the basil and adjust the seasoning, adding salt and pepper if needed.

> **5** Preheat the broiler to high. Drain the monkfish, reserving the marinade. Thread the monkfish and onion alternately onto 4 metal or presoaked wooden skewers.

> **6** Cook the skewers under the preheated broiler, turning occasionally and basting with the reserved marinade, for 6–8 minutes, until golden.

Serve the skewers hot with the basil mayonnaise.

grilled steak
with tomatoes & garlic

serves 4

ingredients

3 tbsp olive oil, plus extra
  for brushing
1 lb 9 oz/700 g tomatoes,
  peeled and chopped
1 red bell pepper, seeded and
  chopped
1 red onion, chopped
2 garlic cloves, finely chopped
1 tbsp chopped fresh
  flat-leaf parsley
1 tsp dried oregano
1 tsp sugar
4 sirloin steaks,
  about 6 oz/175 g each
salt and pepper

> **>1** Place the oil, tomatoes, red bell pepper,
> onion, garlic, parsley, oregano, and sugar
> in a saucepan and season with salt and
> pepper to taste. Bring to a boil, reduce the
> heat, and simmer for 15 minutes.

> **>2** Meanwhile, snip any fat around the
> outsides of the steaks. Season each
> generously with pepper and brush
> with oil.

Transfer the steaks to warmed plates and serve with the tomato-and-garlic sauce.

>3 Heat a ridged grill pan until hot.

>4 Add the steak to the pan and cook according to taste: 2–2½ minutes each side for rare; 3–3½ minutes each side for medium; 4½–5 minutes each side for well done.

baked eggplants with mozzarella & parmesan

serves 6–8

ingredients

3 eggplants, thinly sliced
olive oil, for brushing
10½ oz/300 g mozzarella
 cheese, drained and sliced

1 cup grated Parmesan
 cheese
3 tbsp dried uncolored
 breadcrumbs
1 tbsp butter

tomato & basil sauce
2 tbsp olive oil
4 shallots, finely chopped
2 garlic cloves, finely chopped

14 oz/400 g canned
 plum tomatoes
1 tsp sugar
8 fresh basil leaves, shredded
salt and pepper

> **1** Preheat the oven to 400°F/200°C. Brush an ovenproof dish with oil.

> **2** Arrange the eggplant slices in a single layer on 2 large baking sheets. Brush with oil and bake in the preheated oven for 15–20 minutes, until tender.

> **3** Meanwhile, make the sauce. Heat the oil in a saucepan, add the shallots, and cook for 5 minutes, until softened. Add the garlic and cook for an additional minute.

> **4** Add the tomatoes and break them up with a wooden spoon. Stir in the sugar and season with salt and pepper to taste. Bring to a boil, reduce the heat, and simmer for about 10 minutes, until thickened. Stir in the basil.

>5 Arrange half of the eggplant slices in the bottom of the prepared dish. Cover with half of the mozzarella, spoon over half of the sauce, and sprinkle with half of the Parmesan.

>6 Mix the remaining Parmesan with the breadcrumbs. Repeat the layers, ending with the Parmesan mixture. Dot the top with the butter and bake for 25 minutes, until the topping is golden brown.

Let stand for 5 minutes before serving.

chicken breasts with a parmesan crumb topping

serves 4

ingredients

4 skinless, boneless chicken
  breasts
5 tbsp pesto sauce

¾ cup fresh ciabatta
  breadcrumbs
¼ cup grated Parmesan
  cheese

finely grated rind of ½ lemon
2 tbsp olive oil
salt and pepper
roasted vine tomatoes, to serve

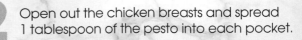
>1 Preheat the oven to 425°F/220°C. Cut a deep slash into each chicken breast to make a pocket.

>2 Open out the chicken breasts and spread 1 tablespoon of the pesto into each pocket.

>3 Fold the chicken flesh back over the pesto and place in an ovenproof dish.

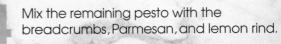
>4 Mix the remaining pesto with the breadcrumbs, Parmesan, and lemon rind.

>5 Spread the breadcrumb mixture over the chicken breasts. Season with salt and pepper to taste and drizzle with the oil.

>6 Bake in the preheated oven for about 20 minutes, or until the juices run clear when a skewer is inserted into the thickest part of the meat.

Serve the chicken hot with roasted vine tomatoes.

sea bass with fennel, olives & thyme

serves 4

ingredients

4 sea bass, about 10½ oz/300 g
  each, cleaned
2 fennel bulbs
12 pitted green olives
juice and finely grated rind
  of 1 lemon
3 tbsp olive oil
¾ cup dry white wine
3 tbsp chopped fresh
  thyme leaves
salt and pepper

>1 Preheat the oven to 400°F/200°C. Cut 3 deep slashes into 1 side of each fish and place in a roasting pan.

>2 Trim the fennel bulbs, reserving the green fronds. Cut into slices about ¼ inch/5 mm thick and blanch in boiling water for 1 minute. Drain and arrange around the fish with the olives.

Transfer to a serving plate and garnish with the reserved fennel fronds.

>3 Lightly whisk together the lemon juice, lemon rind, oil, wine, and thyme with salt and pepper to taste.

>4 Spoon over the fish and fennel, then bake in the preheated oven for 30–35 minutes, until the fish comes away from the bones easily.

deep-fried vegetables with balsamic dip

serves 4

ingredients

about 2 lb/900 g mixed
vegetables, such as fennel,
zucchini, broccoli, cauliflower,
onions, and carrots
scant 1½ cups all-purpose flour

2 eggs, beaten
½ cup beer
olive or vegetable oil,
for deep-frying
salt and pepper

dip

6 tbsp balsamic vinegar
1 tsp mild mustard
1 tsp clear honey

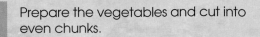>**1** Prepare the vegetables and cut into even chunks.

>**2** Sift the flour into a bowl with salt and pepper to taste. Make a well in the center and add the eggs and beer.

>**3** Stir to mix, then whisk hard to make a smooth, bubbly batter.

>**4** Heat enough oil for deep-frying in a large saucepan or deep-fat fryer to 350–375°F/ 180–190°C, or until a cube of bread browns in 30 seconds. Dip the vegetables in the batter to coat lightly and fry, in batches, until golden brown.

>6 Meanwhile, for the dip, mix together the vinegar, mustard, and honey until smooth.

Serve the vegetables hot with the dip on the side.

duck stew with pancetta, rosemary & olives

serves 4

ingredients

2 tbsp olive oil
4 lb/1.8 kg oven-ready duck,
 cut into 8 pieces
5½ oz/150 g pancetta, diced
1 large onion, diced

1 celery stalk, diced
1 carrot, diced
1 garlic clove, crushed
¾ cup red wine
1¾ cups pureed canned
 tomatoes

1 fresh red chile, finely
 chopped
3 fresh rosemary sprigs
12 black olives
salt and pepper

chopped fresh flat-leaf parsley,
 to garnish

> **1** Heat the oil in a large saucepan and fry the duck pieces, in batches, until golden brown. Remove and set aside.

> **2** Turn out all but 1 tablespoon of the oil and fry the pancetta, stirring, until golden.

> **3** Add the onion, celery, carrot, and garlic and fry gently, stirring, for 3–4 minutes.

> **4** Stir in the wine and boil for 1 minute, then add the pureed tomatoes, chile, rosemary, and olives with salt and pepper to taste.

>5 Return the duck pieces to the saucepan,
spooning over the sauce to cover.

>6 Cover and simmer gently for about
1 hour, or until the duck is tender.

Sprinkle with parsley before serving.

pork with borlotti beans

serves 4

ingredients

1⅓ cups dried borlotti beans, soaked overnight
1 lb 12 oz/800 g pork shoulder
1 large onion, chopped
2 celery stalks, chopped
1 large carrot, chopped
1 fresh red chile, finely chopped
2 garlic cloves, finely chopped
large sprig of each fresh rosemary, thyme, and bay leaves
about 2½ cups chicken stock
salt and pepper
crusty bread, to serve

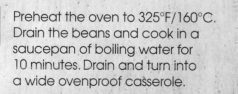

>**1** Preheat the oven to 325°F/160°C. Drain the beans and cook in a saucepan of boiling water for 10 minutes. Drain and turn into a wide ovenproof casserole.

>**2** Cut the pork into bite-size chunks, leaving on any skin.

Serve the pork and beans with chunks of bread to soak up the juices.

>3 Layer the pork and vegetables over the beans, sprinkling the layers with the chile, garlic, and salt and pepper to taste. Tuck in the herb sprigs.

>4 Pour over just enough stock to cover the layers, then cover with the casserole lid and bake in the preheated oven, without stirring, for 3 hours, until tender.

rustic fish casserole

serves 4

ingredients

10½ oz/300 g clams, scrubbed
2 tbsp olive oil
1 large onion, chopped
2 garlic cloves, crushed

2 celery stalks, sliced
12 oz/350 g firm white fish fillet
9 oz/250 g prepared squid rings
1¾ cups fish stock
6 plum tomatoes, chopped

small bunch of fresh thyme
salt and pepper
crusty bread, to serve

1 Clean the clams under cold running water, scrubbing the shells. Discard any with broken shells and any that refuse to close when tapped.

2 Heat the oil in a large pan and fry the onion, garlic, and celery for 3–4 minutes, until softened but not browned.

3 Meanwhile, cut the fish into chunks.

4 Stir the fish and squid into the pan, then fry gently for 2 minutes.

151

> **5** Stir in the stock, tomatoes, and thyme with salt and pepper to taste. Cover and simmer gently for 3–4 minutes.

> **6** Add the clams, cover, and cook over high heat for an additional 2 minutes, or until the shells open. Discard any that remain closed.

Serve the casserole immediately with chunks of bread.

umbrian-style lentils with artichokes

serves 4

ingredients

1 cup French green lentils
2 tbsp olive oil
2 celery stalks, chopped
2 leeks, sliced

1 garlic clove, crushed
1 cup chopped sun-dried
  tomatoes
2 tbsp chopped fresh sage
1 tbsp chopped fresh rosemary

2 cups ham or vegetable stock
10 oz/280 g prepared artichoke
  hearts, drained
salt and pepper

> **1** Place the lentils in a pan and cover with boiling water. Bring to a boil and boil for 10 minutes. Drain and set aside.

> **2** Heat the oil in a large pan and fry the celery and leeks for 2–3 minutes, until softened but not browned.

> **3** Stir in the garlic, sun-dried tomatoes, sage, and rosemary.

> **4** Add the cooked lentils, the stock, and salt and pepper to taste, then bring a boil.

Reduce the heat, cover, and simmer gently for 25–30 minutes, or until the lentils are tender.

>6 Stir in the artichokes and heat gently for 2–3 minutes.

Serve immediately.

grilled tuna with lemon, capers & thyme

serves 4

ingredients

4 tuna steaks,
  about 6 oz/175 g each
4 tbsp olive oil
finely grated rind and juice
  of 1 lemon
3 tbsp salted capers, rinsed
2 tbsp chopped fresh thyme
salt and pepper
lemon wedges, to serve

>1 Brush the tuna steaks with 1 tablespoon of the oil and season with salt and pepper to taste.

>2 Place the remaining oil, the lemon rind and juice, capers, and thyme in a small pan over low heat.

Serve the tuna hot with lemon wedges for squeezing over.

>3 Heat a ridged grill pan until hot, then cook the tuna, in batches if necessary, for 2–3 minutes on each side.

>4 Bring the lemon-and-caper mixture to a boil and spoon over the tuna.

roast lamb with rosemary & marsala

serves 6

ingredients

4 lb/1.8 kg leg of lamb
2 garlic cloves, thinly sliced
2 tbsp rosemary leaves

½ cup olive oil
2 lb/900 g potatoes, cut into
  1-inch/2.5-cm cubes
6 fresh sage leaves, chopped

⅔ cup Marsala
salt and pepper

>1 Preheat the oven to 425°F/220°C. Use a small knife to make incisions all over the lamb, then insert the garlic slices and about half the rosemary leaves.

>2 Place the lamb in a roasting pan and spoon over half the oil. Roast in the preheated oven for 15 minutes.

>3 Reduce the oven temperature to 350°F/180°C. Remove the lamb from the oven and season with salt and pepper to taste. Turn the lamb over, return to the oven, and roast for an additional hour.

>4 Put the potatoes in a separate roasting pan, add the remaining oil, and toss to coat. Sprinkle with the remaining rosemary and the sage. Place the potatoes in the oven with the lamb and roast for 40 minutes.

161

>5 Remove the lamb from the oven, turn it over, and pour over the Marsala. Return it to the oven with the potatoes and cook for an additional 15 minutes.

>6 Transfer the lamb to a carving board and cover with foil. Place the roasting pan over high heat and bring the juices to a boil. Continue to boil until thickened and syrupy.

Carve the lamb into slices and serve with the potatoes and meat juices.

warm vegetable medley

serves 4

ingredients

4 tbsp olive oil
2 celery stalks, sliced
2 red onions, sliced
1 lb/450 g eggplants, diced

1 garlic clove, finely chopped
5 plum tomatoes, chopped
3 tbsp red wine vinegar
1 tbsp sugar
3 tbsp pitted green olives

2 tbsp drained capers
salt and pepper
4 tbsp chopped fresh flat-leaf
  parsley, to garnish
ciabatta bread, to serve

> **1** Heat half the oil in a large heavy-bottom saucepan. Add the celery and onions and cook over low heat, stirring occasionally, for 5 minutes, until softened but not colored.

> **2** Add the remaining oil and the eggplants. Cook, stirring frequently, for about 5 minutes, until the eggplants begin to color.

> **3** Add the garlic, tomatoes, vinegar, and sugar and mix well.

> **4** Cover the mixture with a circle of wax paper and simmer gently for about 10 minutes.

>5 Remove and discard the wax paper, then stir in the olives and capers. Season with salt and pepper to taste.

>6 Turn the mixture into a serving dish and set aside to cool slightly.

Garnish with the parsley and serve
with ciabatta.

beef braised in red wine

serves 4–6

ingredients
2 tbsp olive oil
2 lb 4 oz/1 kg sirloin or top
   round beef, in one piece
1 large onion, sliced
2 carrots, chopped
2 celery stalks, sliced
2 bay leaves
1 cinnamon stick
1¾ cups red wine
1¾ cups beef stock
salt and pepper

>1 Heat the oil in a large saucepan and cook the beef until browned on all sides. Remove the beef from the saucepan and set aside.

>2 Add the onion, carrots, and celery to the saucepan and place the beef on top. Add the bay leaves, cinnamon stick, wine, and stock. Season with salt and pepper to taste.

Carve the beef into slices and serve with the juices poured over.

>3 Bring to a boil and simmer gently, turning the beef occasionally, for about 2 hours, or until tender.

>4 Lift out the beef and keep hot. Strain the juices, then place the saucepan back on the heat and boil rapidly to reduce by about half.

tiramisu

serves 6

ingredients

4 egg yolks
½ cup superfine sugar
1 tsp vanilla extract

2¼ cups mascarpone cheese
2 egg whites
¾ cup strong black coffee
½ cup rum or brandy
24 ladyfingers

2 tbsp unsweetened cocoa
2 tbsp finely grated semisweet
  dark chocolate

>1 Whisk the egg yolks with the sugar and vanilla extract in a heatproof bowl set over a saucepan of barely simmering water.

>2 When the mixture is pale and the whisk leaves a ribbon trail when lifted, remove the bowl from the heat and set aside to cool. Whisk occasionally to prevent a skin from forming.

>3 When the egg yolk mixture is cool, whisk in the mascarpone until thoroughly combined.

>4 Whisk the egg whites in a separate, spotlessly clean bowl until they form soft peaks, then gently fold them into the mascarpone mixture.

173

>5 Combine the coffee and rum in a shallow dish. Briefly dip 8 of the ladyfingers in the mixture, then arrange in the bottom of a serving dish.

>6 Spoon a third of the mascarpone mixture on top, spreading it out evenly. Repeat the layers twice, finishing with the mascarpone mixture. Chill for at least 1 hour.

To serve, sift the cocoa evenly over the top and sprinkle with the chocolate.

ricotta tart with chocolate & walnuts

serves 6

ingredients
generous ½ cup superfine
  sugar
9 tbsp unsalted butter, softened
2 egg yolks
finely grated rind of 1 lemon
2 cups all-purpose flour

filling
4½ oz/125 g semisweet dark
  chocolate, broken into pieces
1 cup ricotta cheese
⅓ cup confectioners' sugar,
  plus extra for dusting
2 tbsp dark rum

1 tsp vanilla extract
¾ cup finely chopped walnuts

> **1** Preheat the oven to 350°F/180°C.
Place the superfine sugar, butter, egg
yolks, and lemon rind in a bowl and
beat well to mix evenly.

> **2** Add the flour and work the mixture with your
fingers to make a smooth dough.

> **3** Wrap the dough in plastic wrap and
let rest at room temperature for about
10 minutes.

> **4** Melt the chocolate in a heatproof bowl set
over a pan of hot water.

>5 Mix together the ricotta, confectioners' sugar, rum, vanilla extract, and walnuts. Stir in the melted chocolate, mixing evenly.

>6 Roll out two-thirds of the dough and press into the bottom and sides of a 9-inch/ 23-cm loose-bottom tart pan.

>7 Spoon the ricotta mixture into the pastry shell, smoothing level.

>8 Roll out the remaining dough, cut into strips, and arrange over the tart to form a lattice. Place on a baking sheet and bake in the preheated oven for 35–40 minutes, until firm and golden.

Serve the tart warm, dusted with confectioners' sugar.

179

stuffed peaches
with amaretto

serves 4

ingredients
4 tbsp unsalted butter
4 peaches
2 tbsp light brown sugar
1 cup crushed amaretti
  cookies
2 tbsp amaretto
½ cup light cream,
  to serve

>1 Preheat the oven to 350°F/180°C.
Grease a baking dish, large
enough to hold 8 peach halves
in a single layer, with 1 tablespoon
of the butter.

>2 Halve the peaches and remove and
discard the pits.

Pour over the amaretto and
serve hot with the cream.

>3 Beat the remaining butter and the sugar
together in a bowl until creamy, add the
cookie crumbs, and mix well.

>4 Arrange the peach halves, cut-side up, in the
prepared baking dish and fill the cavities with
the cookie mixture. Bake in the preheated
oven for 20–25 minutes, or until tender.

almond biscotti

makes about 35

ingredients

1¾ cups whole blanched
   almonds
1⅔ cups all-purpose flour,
   plus extra for dusting

generous ¾ cup superfine
   sugar, plus extra for sprinkling
1 tsp baking powder
½ tsp ground cinnamon
2 eggs
2 tsp vanilla extract

>1 Preheat the oven to 350°F/180°C. Line 2 baking sheets with parchment paper.

>2 Very roughly chop the almonds, leaving some whole.

>3 Mix the flour, sugar, baking powder, and cinnamon together in a mixing bowl. Stir in the almonds.

>4 Beat the eggs with the vanilla extract in a small bowl, then add to the flour mixture and mix together to form a firm dough.

>5 Turn the dough out onto a lightly floured surface and knead lightly.

>6 Divide the dough in half and shape each piece into a log, roughly 2 inches/5 cm wide. Transfer to the prepared baking sheets and sprinkle with sugar. Bake in the preheated oven for 20–25 minutes, until firm.

>7 Remove from the oven and let cool slightly, then transfer to a cutting board and cut into ½-inch/1-cm slices. Meanwhile, reduce the oven temperature to 325°F/160°C.

>8 Arrange the slices, cut-sides down, on the baking sheets. Bake in the oven for 15–20 minutes, until dry and crispy. Transfer to a wire rack to cool.

Store in an airtight container to keep crisp.

venetian-style sweet fritters with candied peel

makes about 24

ingredients

⅔ cup golden raisins
½ cup chopped
  candied peel

3 tbsp grappa or rum
finely grated rind of 1 lemon
3¼ cups all-purpose flour
¼ cup superfine sugar

1 envelope active dry yeast
1 small egg, beaten
about 1 cup lukewarm milk
generous ¼ cup pine nuts

sunflower oil, for deep-frying
confectioners' sugar, for dusting

>1 Place the golden raisins, candied peel, grappa, and lemon rind in a bowl and let soak for 1 hour.

>2 Place the flour, sugar, and yeast in a bowl and stir in the egg with enough of the milk to make a thick batter.

>3 Stir the golden raisin mixture and the pine nuts into the bowl.

>4 Cover and let stand in a warm place for about 3 hours, or until spongy and doubled in size.

>5 Heat enough oil for deep-frying in a large saucepan or deep-fat fryer to 350–375°F/180–190°C, or until a cube of bread browns in 30 seconds.

>6 Drop tablespoons of the batter into the oil and fry until golden. Drain on paper towels.

Serve the fritters hot, dusted with confectioners' sugar.

peach compote with limoncello

serves 4

ingredients
4 peaches
⅓ cup superfine sugar
1 cinnamon stick
3 tbsp cold water
2 tbsp limoncello liqueur
whipped cream, to serve

>1 Cut the peaches in half and remove the pits.

>2 Place the peaches in a wide pan with the sugar, cinnamon stick, and water. Bring to a boil.

Serve the compote warm or
cold with whipped cream.

>3 Cover and cook over low heat, stirring
occasionally, for 10 minutes, or until the
peaches are tender.

>4 Remove from the heat, stir in
the limoncello, and let stand
for 20 minutes before serving.

fig tartlets

serves 4

ingredients

9 oz/250 g store-bought
  puff pastry
all-purpose flour, for dusting
8 fresh ripe figs

1 tbsp superfine sugar
½ tsp ground cinnamon
milk, for brushing
vanilla ice cream, to serve

> **1** Preheat the oven to 375°F/190°C. Roll out the pastry on a lightly floured surface to a thickness of ¼ inch/5 mm.

> **2** Using a saucer as a guide, cut out four 6-inch/15-cm rounds and place on a baking sheet.

> **3** Use a sharp knife to score a line halfway through each pastry round, about ½ inch/1 cm from the outer edge. Prick the center all over with a fork.

> **4** Slice the figs into quarters and arrange 8 quarters over the center of each pastry round.

>5 Mix together the sugar and cinnamon and sprinkle over the figs.

>6 Brush the edges of the pastry with milk and bake in the preheated oven for 15–20 minutes, until risen and golden brown.

Serve the tartlets warm with ice cream.

tuscan christmas cake

serves 14

ingredients

¾ cup hazelnuts
¾ cup almonds
½ cup chopped candied
  peel

⅓ cup finely chopped
  plumped dried apricots
⅓ cup finely chopped candied
  pineapple
grated rind of 1 orange

½ cup all-purpose flour
2 tbsp unsweetened cocoa
1 tsp ground cinnamon
¼ tsp ground coriander
¼ tsp freshly grated nutmeg

¼ tsp ground cloves
generous ½ cup superfine
  sugar
¾ cup honey
confectioners' sugar, for dusting

> **1** Preheat the oven to 350°F/180°C. Line an 8-inch/20-cm round springform cake pan with parchment paper.

> **2** Spread out the hazelnuts on a baking sheet and toast in the preheated oven for 10 minutes, until golden brown. Turn them onto a dish towel and rub off the skins.

> **3** Meanwhile, spread out the almonds on a baking sheet and toast in the oven for 10 minutes, until golden. Watch carefully because they can burn easily.

> **4** Reduce the oven temperature to 300°F/150°C. Chop all the nuts and place in a large bowl. Add the candied peel, apricots, pineapple, and orange rind to the nuts and mix well.

> **5** Sift the flour, cocoa, cinnamon, coriander, nutmeg, and cloves into the bowl and mix well.

> **6** Put the superfine sugar and honey into a saucepan and set over low heat, stirring, until the sugar has dissolved. Bring to a boil and cook for 5 minutes, until thickened and beginning to darken.

> **7** Stir the nut mixture into the saucepan and remove from the heat.

> **8** Spoon the mixture into the prepared cake pan and smooth the surface. Bake in the oven for 1 hour, then transfer to a wire rack to cool. When cold, carefully remove from the pan and peel off the parchment paper.

To serve, dust the top of the cake with confectioners' sugar and cut into thin wedges.

zabaglione

serves 4

ingredients
4 egg yolks
⅓ cup superfine sugar
5 tbsp Marsala
amaretti cookies, to serve

>1 Whisk the egg yolks with the sugar in a
heatproof bowl for about 1 minute.

>2 Gently whisk in the Marsala.

Serve with amaretti cookies.

>3 Set the bowl over a saucepan of barely simmering water and whisk vigorously for 10–15 minutes, until thick, creamy, and foamy.

>4 Immediately pour into serving glasses.

sweet cheese ravioli with honey

serves 4

ingredients

1⅔ cups type 00 pasta flour or all-purpose flour, plus extra for dusting

⅓ cup superfine sugar
2 eggs, beaten
¾ cup coarsely grated pecorino cheese

4 tbsp light olive oil
6 tbsp flower honey
ground cinnamon, for sprinkling

>1 Sift the flour and sugar into a bowl and make a well in the center.

>2 Add the eggs and stir with a fork to gradually incorporate the dry ingredients into the eggs to form a dough.

>3 Turn out the dough onto a lightly floured surface and knead gently until smooth.

>4 Roll out the dough to a thickness of about ⅛ inch/3 mm. Use a 3¼-inch/8-cm cutter to stamp out 24 rounds.

>5 Divide the pecorino between 12 of the dough rounds.

>6 Brush the edges with water and top with the remaining rounds, pressing the edges to seal.

>7 Heat the oil in a skillet until moderately hot but not smoking, then fry the ravioli, in batches if necessary, for 1½–2 minutes on each side, until golden.

>8 Gently warm the honey in a small saucepan and drizzle over the ravioli.

Sprinkle the ravioli with cinnamon and serve hot.

cornmeal & almond cake

serves 6

ingredients

scant 1 cup unsalted butter, softened

1 cup superfine sugar

juice and finely grated rind of 1 small orange

3 eggs, beaten

2¼ cups ground almonds

1⅔ cups instant cornmeal

1 tsp baking powder

vanilla ice cream, to serve

> **1** Preheat the oven to 350°F/180°C. Grease a 9-inch/23-cm round cake pan with a little of the butter and line the bottom with parchment paper.

> **2** Beat together the remaining butter and the sugar with an electric mixer until pale and fluffy.

> **3** Add the orange juice and rind, eggs, and almonds. Sift in the cornmeal and baking powder and beat until smooth.

> **4** Spread the mixture in the prepared pan, smoothing with a palette knife.

>5 Bake in the preheated oven for 35–40 minutes, until firm and golden. Remove from the oven and let cool in the pan for 20 minutes.

>6 Transfer the cake to a wire rack to cool.

Cut the cake into slices and serve warm or cold with ice cream.

prosecco sorbet
with grapes

serves 4

ingredients
¾ cup superfine sugar
⅔ cup water
thinly pared strip of lemon zest
juice of 1 lemon
1½ cups prosecco
grapes and fresh mint sprigs,
  to decorate

 >1 Place the sugar and water in a pan with the lemon zest.

>2 Stir over low heat until the sugar dissolves, then boil for 2–3 minutes to reduce by half. Let cool and remove the lemon zest.

Decorate with grapes and
mint sprigs before serving.

>3 Combine the syrup with the lemon juice
and prosecco, then churn the mixture
in an ice-cream maker following the
manufacturer's directions. Alternatively,
pour into a freezerproof container and
freeze, uncovered, whisking at hourly
intervals until frozen.

>4 When ready to serve, let stand at room
temperature to soften slightly, then scoop
the sorbet into sundae glasses.

panna cotta with spiced plums

serves 4

ingredients

panna cotta
4 leaves gelatin
1¼ cups milk

1 cup mascarpone cheese
½ cup superfine sugar
1 vanilla bean, halved
  lengthwise

spiced plums
8 red plums, halved and pitted
3 tbsp honey
1 cinnamon stick

thinly pared strip of orange zest
1 tbsp balsamic vinegar

>**1** Soak the gelatin leaves in ¼ cup of the milk for 10 minutes.

>**2** Place the remaining milk, the mascarpone, sugar, and vanilla bean in a saucepan and heat gently, stirring until smooth, then bring to a boil.

>**3** Remove from the heat, discard the vanilla bean, and add the gelatin mixture, stirring until completely dissolved.

>**4** Pour into four 1-cup individual pudding molds. Let chill in the refrigerator until set.

>5 Place the plums, honey, cinnamon stick, orange zest, and vinegar in a pan, cover, and cook gently for 10 minutes, or until the plums are tender.

>6 Dip the bottom of each mold quickly in hot water and turn out onto a serving plate.

Serve the panna cotta with the spiced
plums on the side.

sicilian ice cream

serves 6–8

ingredients

1¾ cups ricotta cheese
1½ cups confectioners' sugar
1 tsp orange flower water

scant 1 cup heavy cream
scant ⅔ cup chopped
  candied peel
⅓ cup chopped angelica

⅓ cup chopped candied
  cherries
1½ oz/40 g semisweet dark
  chocolate, chopped

⅓ cup chopped pistachio nuts
candied fruit, to serve

>1 Press the ricotta through a strainer into a bowl using a wooden spoon.

>2 Stir in the confectioners' sugar and orange flower water, beating until smooth.

>3 Whip the cream until thick enough to hold its shape, then fold into the ricotta mixture.

>4 Churn in an ice-cream maker or freeze in a freezerproof container until slushy.

>5 Fold in the candied peel, angelica, candied cherries, chocolate, and pistachio nuts.

>6 Turn the mixture into a 5-cup/1.2-liter bombe mold or bowl and freeze until firm. Let stand at room temperature for 10–15 minutes before turning out.

Cut the ice cream into wedges and serve with candied fruit.

lemon granita

serves 4

ingredients
scant 2 cups water
scant ⅔ cup granulated sugar
1 cup lemon juice
grated rind of 1 lemon

>1 Heat the water in a heavy-bottom saucepan over low heat. Add the sugar and stir until it has dissolved. Bring to a boil, then remove from the heat and let cool.

>2 Stir the lemon juice and rind into the cooled syrup.

Spoon into sundae glasses
and serve immediately.

>3 Pour the mixture into a freezerproof
container and freeze for 3–4 hours.

>4 Remove the container from the freezer and
dip the bottom into hot water. Turn out the
ice block and chop roughly, then place in a
heavy-duty food processor and process until
it forms small crystals.

Index